Colors
IN NATURE

Albatros

Contents

Prelude

Who painted the trees green? Well, nature can do this and other magic. Nature abounds in colors of all shades. Long, long ago, people began to name colors after plants, animals, and minerals they saw them in to better tell them apart. But as time passed, ever more plants, animals, and minerals were discovered that reminded us of colors already named. So we started to use the names for shades we already knew to name these new natural elements. What are these names? Join us as we look at beautiful color shades one by one—from snow white to canary yellow, ruby red to forget-me-not blue and moss green to the blackest black, dark as the night sky. On each spread, some shades can be connected to a particular plant, animal, or a stone you can find in the picture. Can you match these colors with the corresponding object?

Moon

coconut

opal

collared dove eggs

almonds

moonstone

snowy owl

rock crystal

rock salt

cashmere goat

great egret

Dall sheep

cabbage white

chamomile

lily of the valley

mute swan

daisy

cotton plant

spiny dye-murex

champignon mushroom

Arctic white

pure white

snow white

daisy white

seashell white

cream white

white stork

birch

limestone

ox-eye daisy

field bindweed

diamond

dandelion seedhead

alabaster

jasmine

White

White—how lightly it moves!
A plump *cloud* in the sky, whitish *dandelion fluff* …
Little fragile parachute, whither with the white?
On a snowstorm, with the clink of *icicles* …
Far, far away! To where *snowflakes* dance.

white water lily

black-headed gull

snowflakes

Arctic fox

shell with pearl

dandelion fluffy parachutes

icicles

polar bear

Arctic hare

young harbor seal

ice floe

almond white

coconut white

alabaster white

eggshell white

pearl white

ivory white

siskin

plumeria

amber

ramaria

waxcap

sulphur

gold

forsythia

yellow umbrella stick

great tit

vanilla

wild daffodil

Danube clouded yellow

eyelash viper

cowslip

honey

yellow pea

honey bee

corn

pineapple

ginger

banana

lemon

lady's-slipper orchid

vanilla yellow

banana yellow

canary yellow

lemon yellow

daffodil yellow

sun yellow

8

Yellow

Yellow smiles like a *sunflower* in bloom.
Buzzes like a *bumblebee* in flight.
Shimmers, too. And warms like the *sunrays*
that tickle your face each morning.

Sun

Atlantic canary

citrine

baby chicks

yellow crocus

lesser celandine

bumblebee

mimosa

golden oriole

golden frog

kingcup

yellow swallontail

copperband butterflyfish

bluecheek butterflyfish

sunflower

yellow wagtail

yellow tang

golden tanager

dandelion

22-spot ladybird

honey yellow

sunflower yellow

gold

dandelion yellow

amber yellow

corn yellow

9

peregrine falcon

long-eared owl

cross spider

giant peacock moth

grove snail

desert sand

chamois

bonga

antelope

African forest buffalo

giraffe

Bactrian camel

forester kangaroo

forest bonga

lion

brown owl

roe deer

red deer hind

Eurasian lynx

barley

red deer

red deer calf

tree sparrow

beige

tan

caramel brown

straw brown

fawn brown

sand brown

10

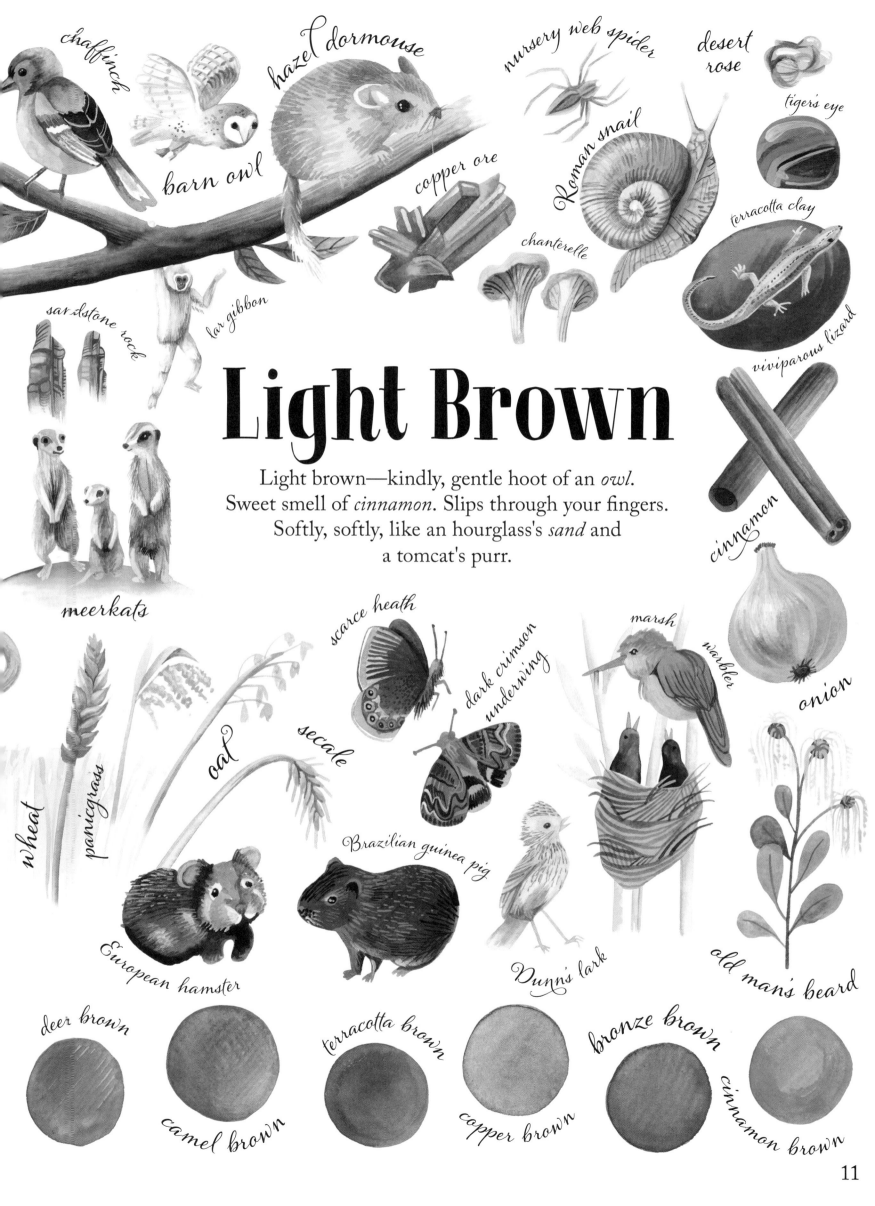

chaffinch

hazel dormouse

barn owl

nursery web spider

desert rose

tiger's eye

copper ore

Roman snail

terracotta clay

chanterelle

sandstone rock

lar gibbon

viviparous lizard

Light Brown

Light brown—kindly, gentle hoot of an *owl*.
Sweet smell of *cinnamon*. Slips through your fingers.
Softly, softly, like an hourglass's *sand* and
a tomcat's purr.

cinnamon

onion

meerkats

scarce heath

dark crimson underwing

marsh warbler

wheat

panicgrass

oat

secale

Brazilian guinea pig

European hamster

Dunn's lark

old man's beard

deer brown

camel brown

terracotta brown

copper brown

bronze brown

cinnamon brown

peach

Hokkaido pumpkin

hooded oriole

common blanketflower

red siskin

golden lion tamarin

angel's trumpets

fox

small tortoiseshell

Hawaii akepa

squirrel

Bengal tiger

orange day-lily

pot marigold

fire opal

orange coneflower

common clownfish

Alpine newt

papaya

coral

tangerine

peach orange

coral orange

carrot orange

papaya orange

apricot orange

fire opal

garden tiger moth

autumn leaves

Eurasian hoopoe

flame bowerbird

apricot

sun parakeet

Cape gooseberry

Orange

Orange dances in a whirl of *autumn leaves*,
in fiery sparks of evening sun,
the sweet taste of *oranges* on your lips,
swallowing what remains of summer.

Gulf fritillary

persimmon

Natal lily

orange

Turk's cap lily

orange-cheeked waxbill

butterfly weed

rufous hummingbird

carrot

slug

tangerine orange

orange

pumpkin orange

persimmon orange

rust orange

marigold orange

goji

raspberry

hibiscus

scarlet tanager

bullfinch

red admiral

goldfinch

red-throated twinspot

cardinal

Japanese macaque

crimson finch

red-capped robin

seven-spot ladybird

American robin

cherries

red panda

dog rose

rowan

wine grapes

strawberry

fly amanita

dog rose flower

red poppy

tomato red

strawberry red

raspberry red

cherry red

ruby red

wine red

14

dawn

ruby

cinnabar

bull's eye

garnet

red aventurine

carnelian

Papuan king parrot

robin redbreast

jasper

ruby-throated hummingbird

beadlet anemone

Mediterranean red star

peacock butterfly

Red

Red glows from meadows and fields through blooming *poppies*. Charmed into *ladybird* wings, crossing plains of red *roses*, ending on hands sweet with the juice of fresh-picked *strawberries*—palms that bloom in fairy-tale love.

cranberry

chili pepper

red apple

radish

watermelon

grapefruit

tomato

beetroot

pomegranate

crimson red

garnet red

burgundy

fiery red

scarlet red

cinnabar red

pink agate

rosewood

fuchsia

magnolia

rosy starling

hedgehog coneflower

common fumitory

rose mallow

cherry tree

Gallic rose

martagon lily

ragged-robin

Nubian bee-eater

moth orchid

dame's rocket

tea rose

Anna's hummingbird

common mallow

pink robin

cyclamen

plumeless thistles

foxglove

begonia

common corncockle

Japanese cherry

misty rose

cherry blossom pink

flamingo pink

rose pink

mauve

thistle

16

salmon

axolotl

octopus

Amazon
river dolphin

galah

stalagmites

jellyfish

common
starfish

anemone

common
sea urchin

Mediterranean scallop

Pink

Pink—snug in the down of *spring birds*,
shimmering under eyelids,
fragrant with *blossoms* of lone wayside *cherries*.
Pink delicateness of *flamingo* wings.

rose quartz

viburnum
farreri

lotus

oleander

cattleya

common
verbena

clover

cushion pink

cobweb
house-leek

Caribbean flamingo

fuchsia

rosewood pink

salmon

orchid pink

cyclamen pink

begonia pink

17

amethyst

eggplant

blackberry

violet-eared waxbill

violet turaco

purple honeycreeper

elderberry

Japanese wisteria

dense blazing star

sweet scabious

spring crocus

purple archangel

alfalfa

purplehead barb

Siberian iris

violet-headed hummingbird

purple sea urchin

crowned woodnymph

fluorite

wild thyme

dates

fig

heather

blackberry

lilac

lavender

iris

amethyst

violet

purple-throated carib

wood violet

pasque flower

plum

violet-backed starling

lavender

lungwort

garden hyacinth

vine grapes

early-purple orchid

rosemary

heartsease

giant onion

purple-throated woodstar

Alpine aster

Purple

Purple breathes fragrant *lavender* desire.
Taste the sweet yet tart *grapes of the vine*?
Come evening, *violets* close their heavy flowers,
to tempt with dreams of journeys unknown,
and mouths filled with *blackberries*.

violet cuckoo

hortensia

thyme

lilac

elderberry

eggplant

plum

purple

mulberry

heather violet

lapis lazuli

turquoise

sapphire

indigo bunting

blue morpho butterfly

Mazarine blue

two-leaf squill

azure lake

liverleaf

bluebell

lesser periwinkle

river kingfisher

cornflower

baby blue eyes

chicory

wood forget-me-not

large-leaved lupine

mallard

flax

grape hyacinth

hyacinth macaw

blueberries

forget-me-not blue

sky blue

cornflower blue

azure blue

turquoise

ocean blue

20

wood nuthatch

blue tit

aquamarine

barn swallow

blue peafowl

blue jay

prunus spinosa

stemless gentian

Blue

Blue, flashing in a preening *peacock's* crown,
flowing wild in a *mountain stream*.
Laying on *bilberried* lips a taste of salt,
crystals from deep, dark blue *oceans*,
infinite mirrors of the skies.

chalcedony

blue hawker

red-cheeked cordonbleu

true forget-me-not

ocean

harlequin duck

blue tang

bowhead whale

aquamarine blue

sapphire blue

whale blue

peacock blue

indigo

teal

21

nepenthes

avocado

kiwi

lime

green olives

red-eyed treefrog

mistletoe

tea tree

birch

veiled chameleon

budgerigar

green-breasted mango

European green woodpecker

day gecko

western green mamba

green sea turtle

Nile crocodile

saguaro cactus

prickly pear

common haircap

bamboo

Venus flytrap

aloe vera

nettle

wood sorrel

ferns

pistachios

couch grass

orchard grass

blue grass

field horsetail

European tree frog

European eel

common carp

northern pike

jade green

linden green

mint

Pistachio

apple green

olive green

22

European mantis

jade

maple

emerald

acorns

violet-green swallow

beech

oak

fir

malachite

littleleaf linden

Green

Green *apple* leaves smile out from gardens.
Forests lush with rain rustle green near and far.
Green *frogs* croak green songs to *carps*.
Forest, garden, and mystery of green *moss*, they
all fall down to the pool's bottom.

apple tree

mint

basil

asparagus

broccoli

lettuce

common green bottle fly

cucumber

parsley

pear

pea

cabbage

spinach

zucchini

artichoke

lime green

emerald green

pine green

grass green

fir green

moss green

griffon vulture

coconut

cocoa tree

walnut

hazelnut

northern goshawk

Sunda slow loris

crested tit

pine cone

smoky quartz

brown earth

elk

red-backed shrike

larch

Bornean orangutan

coyote

European bison

ochre rock

greylag goose

reed bunting

reed

mahogany

Eurasian beaver

Arabian horse

common viper

cocoa brown

ochre

coconut brown

coyote brown

coffee brown

earth brown

common buzzard

coffee tree

coffee beans

pine marten

quail

reindeer

pheasant

brown hare

acorns

beech nuts

chestnuts

brown bear

parasol mushroom

petrified wood

fireflies

cockchafer

long-eared owl

Eurasian hobby

Eurasian skylark

European hedgehog

summer cep

song thrush

spruce cone

Brown

Brown is a heavily plowed field,
wrinkled body of centenarian oak,
moist *earth* prepared for sowing.
Hear the *horse's* thunderous hooves?
Brown—silk-soft in a cup of chocolate.

chocolate brown

chestnut brown

mahogany brown

walnut brown

beaver brown

khaki

basalt rock

great grey owl

common long-eared bat

rock pigeon

grey-headed myna

goat willow catkins

grey squirrel

house mouse

European mole

feather agate

falcon eye stone

fat dormouse

donkey

grey heron

badger

collared dove

elephant

Miss Willmott's ghost

common cuckoo

hook-lipped rhinoceras

ostrich

grey-headed woodpecker

silver

dove grey

agate grey

ash grey

pebble grey

dolphin grey

koala

grey agate

harbor seal

bottlenose dolphin

pebbles

California sea lion

dudleya succulent

agave

swordfish

sea trout

great white shark

smooth hammerhead

granite

Grey

Make your way through the fog,
grey and thick as fresh-drawn milk.
Step with care on a beach of *pebbles* smooth and wet,
printing their stories on your soles—stories once
whispered among *dolphins*.

lichens

hippopotamus

ring-tailed lemur

silver

mandrill

lead

Linne's two-toed sloth

olive baboon

wildcat

grey wolf

mouse grey

squirrel grey

lichen grey

basalt grey

lead grey

taupe

coal

hematite

snowflake obsidian

graphite

great spotted woodpecker

midnight sky

onyx

blackbird

Dalmatian jasper

fire salamander

peewit

black scorpion

Mexican redknee tarantula

slate

black woodpecker

stag beetle

field cricket

starling

Ceylon ebony

carabus coriaceus

black curran

black olives

common magpie

orca

manta ray

black coral

black bean

graphite black

anthracite

raven black

charcoal

black lava

crow black

28

blackcap

house martin

common swift

anthracite

wild yak

capercaillie

red wood ant

rook

crow

panda

Black

Black is a *night* that has lost its stars,
and a day under a cloak.
Flooded with ink and wrapped in *coal*,
a soft caw-cawing from underneath,
while in the field the hungry *rook* pecks
a frozen clod.

emperor penguin

black-and-white ruffed lemur

emperor tamarin

common mussel

black panther

western gorilla

plains zebra

ebony

black bean

black olive

ink black

midnight black

slate black

Mixing Colors

purple

red

orange

blue

In order to create new colors, you need to mix two *primary colors* together. Red and yellow makes orange, yellow and blue creates green, and mixing red and blue yields purple.

green

yellow

By adding the color white, you can make colors *lighter* …

… and by adding black, you can make them *darker*.

You can try mixing colors on your own;
just follow these advanced recipes:

× **7** + × **1** + × **1** = almond white

× **2** + × **2** + × **1** = straw brown

× **3** + × **2** + × **2** = apricot orange

× **3** + × **2** + × **1** = lavender

× **6** + × **3** + × **2** = turquoise

× **3** + × **3** + × **1** = lime green

× **7** + × **5** + × **2** = chestnut brown

turquoise

chestnut brown

lime green

almond white

lavender

apricot orange

straw brown

© Designed by B4U Publishing for Albatros,
an imprint of Albatros Media Group, 2021.
Na Pankráci 30, Prague 4, Czech Republic
Authors: Jana Sedláčková, Štěpánka Sekaninová
Illustrator: Magdalena Konečná
Printed in Czech Republic by Tiskárna Helbich, a.s.
ISBN 978-80-00-05933-4